**See M**

Ellen

MW00487907

 **Rigby**

A Harcourt Achieve Imprint

www.Rigby.com

1-800-531-5015

See me work.

My job is to dig holes.

See me work.

My job is to help pets.

See me work.

My job is to paint pictures.

See me work.

My job is to drive trucks.

See me work.

My job is to bake cakes.

See me work.

My job is to pick fruit.

13

See me work.

My job is to build houses.

See me work.
My job is to teach!